Volume 1

2014-15

cover image by Deborah Ann Dawson

Cobra Lily is a review of art and literature, focusing on the cultural and natural environs of Southwest Oregon. We seek to promote voices from the region, as well as voices outside the area which speak to the natural rhythms and experience of life here. We publish occasionally on the web, as well as an annual print edition (which you likely hold in your hands or tablet).

Why Cobra Lily? The carnivorous pitcher plant exists most abundantly in Southwest Oregon. This native plant has distinctively adapted to thrive in our region. We draw inspiration from this plant because we dare to be as unique, publishing the diverse writers and artists of Southwest Oregon's extraordinary landscape and culture.

We accept poetry, fiction, memoir, essays, regional history, interviews with interesting locals, photography, paintings, and more (i.e. don't feel you need to limit yourself to these genre categories/suggestions). Work can be emailed to us at cobralilyreview@gmail.com.

Deadline to submit is February 15.

We consider previously published material, but please notify where/when it was published previously and make sure you have the rights to republish. Also at this point (and possibly for every point going forward), we are unable to pay for work. Please don't take this as a commentary on the value of your work.

Simultaneous submissions are encouraged (you have to get your stuff out there), but please let us know immediately if someone else accepts your work and you need to withdraw the work (and then accept our congratulations).

Finally, please remember that we are a journal focused on the culture and nature of Southwest Oregon, so in your email/letter, we'd appreciate if you could share the connection to the region of your work and/or yourself. (Even if your work was just formed while passing through the area, we'd still love to see it.) Thank you for your interest.

- Ryan Forsythe & Michael Spring, Editors

ISSN 2377-1550

Published by Left Fork Books of O'Brien, Oregon

Contents

Gary Lark 6 Snake Road
7 Lost
8 The Advice is Free
Pepper Trail 9 The Commerce of the Mountain
10 In an Aspen Grove
Melissa Matthewson 12 A Country Wedding
Patty Wixon 14 Early April
Scott T. Starbuck 15 Earth Like a Deck of a Ship
'Buckwheat Bob' Harrison 16 The Freeze
John Noland 25 Earth Music
26 Sea Riddles and Doorways
Rhonda Lynn 27 Fiber Arts
Lilyana Rain 30 Wonder
Kindi Fahrnkopf 32 Thunder Warning
33 Rain
Kay Elaine Ekwall 34 In the Soft Silence
Dave Dunbar 36 Troutish Longings
Kelly Waldin 38 My tribe is getting smaller.
Anita Savio 39 Night Visions
Rich Norman 44 Poem for Paul
David Lorenz Winston 47 Nature Photography
Dallion McGregor 50 Full Moon Meditation
Summer Wolf 51 Finding Me
52 Writing
Juliette Wolf 53 Great Big Cedar
Isaac Wolf 53 The Cave

Contents

David Newell 54 Eyes Slide Off of Me
54 The Poem Said
55 My Life
55 I Gotta Go to the Ocean
56 The Poem Said
Susan Gustafson 57 The Date to Hell…and Back Again
Angela Graves 59 R.I.P Blaze
Annette McGee Rasch 60 Of Women and Mice
63 Big Brothers for Cows
Michael Spring 65 Cobra Lily
Savanna G. S. 66 Teardrops from the Clouds
Alan Laurie 67 Winter Solstice Mandala
68 Electric Mandala
Sara Backer 69 I Like Coffee
70 Redwood Vision
71 Weeder Geese
72 The Rabbit
73 Four Senryu for the Beaver
Scott Simpson 74 If . . . (Doghouse)
Rory Forsythe-Elder 76 Wolves
Deborah Ann Dawson 77 Lady of the Lake
78 Door in the River
79 Silent Among the Reeds
Kathryn Velho 80 Anabel
Kailen Forsythe-Elder 82 Taped Pumpkin

Gary Lark

Snake Road

There's a hammer on the floor
sliding on sharp curves.
A shovel plays hockey with beer cans
in the pickup bed,
goal posts changing down the snake road.
What you don't understand
goes better with speed—
feeling the pull of inertia,
the rev and push of a good engine,
almost in control.
I'm driving into foreign land.
Gravel flies as I ride the ridges
past everything I know.

Lost

It was somewhere between
dusk and dark
on a road off another road
when I saw a blur
coming full tilt
up along the river
growing into a deer.
I thought it was going to run right into us.
As it briefly gathered its power
to clear the car
I could see velvet covered horns,
its determined line of grace.
We had stopped
to figure out where we were,
headlights still on,
door cracked
for the dome light
on our map,
a soft cottonwood smell
filling the night.
I looked up
to see where the color changes
from side hair to belly hair,
the fine texture
forming runs and swirls
and legs passing over.

The Advice is Free

Nobody lives up that way.
You can drive up there
clear to the end of the road
where the bridge crosses
Widow Creek for the last time
but there's nobody up there.
Look here on the map,
see where it dead ends,
there's a gravel quarry
on the west side
and up here is where the mill used to sit.
Go up there if you like
but when the mill shut down
everybody moved out,
except the Peabody's,
now they're gone too.
That'll be twelve dollars for the gas.

Gary Lark's work includes *Without a Map* (Wellstone Press, 2013), *Getting By*, winner of the Holland Prize from Logan House Press, 2009, and three chapbooks. His work has appeared in *Beloit Poetry Journal*, *Hubbub*, *Poet Lore*, and *The Sun*. Three poems were featured on The Writer's Almanac with Garrison Keillor. He and his wife Dorothy live in the Rogue Valley.

The Commerce of the Mountain

The bumblebee, squat and hairy bagman, trundles around his neighborhood, one flower to the nearby next, filling his sacks with gold, humming to himself all the while. On a fine August day, there is no more self-satisfied citizen on the mountain.

The warblers are in motley now, their badges of black and yellow worn to tatters, the dramas of song, courtship, nest and eggs and hungry mouths forgotten, mingling in the ragamuffin democracy of migration, nothing left to fight for and enough for all.

The hummingbird harbors still his zest for rage, his blood hot, his pride easily pricked, his honor forever to be defended. Lord of his patch of penstamon, he is on the dash, looking for trouble, flashing his sword, seeking a challenger, exulting in heat, and sugar, and speed.

Overhead, the vulture walks the tightrope of sky, balances on dark wings, ignorant of flowers, disinterested in bumblebees, hummingbirds, warblers, all too small in death to reach him with news of their decay, blind to the bright, with no taste for the sweet, meadowless and alone.

In an Aspen Grove

Here I was born, October, my month
Season of fruition and the fall
Beginning from here, I grew
In some ways changed, but always
Remained and am, here, now, on this rock,
One

One body, one mind despite its disarray
One set of legs that pull me through
The world, one pair of hands to grasp
And feed my one hungry mouth
Within these trees, how strange to be
Alone

The aspens are a multitude, each
A clone, the grove an acre of organism
Most living, some few dead, breaking and rotting
Feeding the colony that lives, sends roots
Into the soft fallen bodies that thus regain
The many

Above my head, the leaves, particulates of light
Forever tremble, shiver the blue sky to shards
Golden and golden green, each limb hundreds
Each tree thousands, each gust sending more
West across the meadow, burning, then quenched
In shadow

And with the light the sound, ceaseless
Rustle and murmuration, the bare white
Noise of wind tuned by turning leaves
To sense, to conversation, to the hubbub
Of a community conversing in harmony
With itself

O, how lonely it is to be
In the aspen grove dark
Beneath those golden leaves
Speechless within that confabulation
Needing everything, and always
Only one

Pepper Trail's poetry has appeared in *Comstock Review, Atlanta Review, Spillway, Turtle Island Quarterly, Toe Good Poetry, Windfall*, and other publications, and his poem "Syllabus for the Warming World" was recently nominated for a Pushcart Prize by *Cascadia Review*. His environmental essays have been a regular feature of the *Jefferson Monthly*'s "Jefferson Almanac" since 1997. Trail lives in Ashland, Oregon, where he works for the U.S. Fish and Wildlife Service.

Melissa Matthewson

A Country Wedding

We walked our rural road on a Saturday, the pavement saturated with the day's rain and littered with leaves shuffled from the trees at odds with the hardy west wind. Our daughter wore a brown dress speckled with white shapes like triangles, brown tights to match and pink shoes. She was pretty with tiny braids wrapped on top of her head, the rest of her auburn curls falling to the straight line above her hips. Our son held my hand, skipped along with his nice clothes and missing teeth lost now to the spaces in his grin like open doorways. As we walked, you told me of your dream: about a woman who took you to dinner, a woman not your wife, a woman not me. Your father disapproved of this handing you cigarettes and said, "Smoke them or don't," and you laughed in the re-telling while we walked under the heavy sky with the sun splintering the day with so much clear light, strips of ribbon we could walk through on our way to the next farm over for a country wedding at the tip of autumn.

Funny how our dreams become laughter or story to fill our talk, our time together.

There were children everywhere in the wet grass when we arrived, and too, a pig roasting in a box, an arbor made of madrone branches, a band coiling wires. We said hello to our neighbors and made acquaintance with the new. I eyed a young man in a floppy hat looking like something straight out of a hay pile. He asked me to dance later when you disappeared to the pie or trees where our son chased other boys down by the black creek. I can't lie—dancing with another man under the moon was dangerous and enchanting, so true in its simple shape of attraction, of desire, of want.

The officiant told a story. He said, "This story might be true, but it might not. I'm not concerned with the facts." He told of the Grand Canyon, the layers of rock compared to a marriage over time—the soft new love of the rudimentary bands to the deeper depths of rock where intimacy lives. I held your hand while the bride smiled in her sheen and silk dress of blue with an

appliqué of branches and tree swirling around the hem and up through the bodice, a broach of diamonds at her split of breasts and flowers in her hair, of course. The groom wore pants of buckskin sewed at night in his cabin, his muscle and bone sliding into the leather so effortlessly like he was born into them. He was barefoot in the clover.

I drank too much hard cider brewed by the apple farmers up the road while the band played music that carried me away under the silver clouds shifting and mixing in the aftermath of the earlier storm. The string lights overhead cast a glow about the place that made every shadow count, illuminating the cheeks of all the people who sipped and talked and celebrated. The light made us all beautiful.

Later, we swayed back down our road way too late with that harvest moon peeking through the clouds and our children thought I was silly because I chattered on about the essay I was writing, a rejoinder to a rejoinder, and how we were to make an experiment with eggs in the morning. I rambled all this while I pushed them in the stroller, heavy with umbrellas, sweaters and pouches of lavender, party favors we could tuck under our pillows when we arrived home. They didn't understand my slur and stream of words and said, "Mamaaaaa," all drawn out and laughing. I wished for them to remember this laughing, this joy.

That's when the clouds parted and our field came into view, bare now after having been mowed that morning, and our farm looked as if it were a bowl, the beauty difficult to describe even, but I felt it pulling us toward it, this container of our life, and of many things, like love and work and some day, death. I saw the field washed in moon glow, fine and bright and everything we keep was revealed to me as I tipped over sideways from the cider, the music, the marrying.

I think, I'm writing this now so I'll remember what I feel about this place that holds so much for us. So I'll remember it wasn't just a dream we laughed about once when we were young and buoyant and drunk on mountain cider. I think, I'm writing this for you. So you'll know.

Melissa Matthewson's essays have appeared, or are forthcoming, in *River Teeth*, *Defunct*, *Numero Cinq*, *Pithead Chapel*, *Under the Gum Tree*, *Terrain*, *Prime Number*, and *Literary Mama* among other publications. She is currently pursuing an MFA in creative nonfiction from the Vermont College of Fine Arts. She lives on an organic vegetable farm in the Applegate Valley. Find her at melissamatthewson.com or on twitter at @melmatthewson.

Patty Wixon

Early April

1.
At the Pacific's edge, we looked toward the horizon
seeming flat, then starting a steady rise, relentless
building toward the smash against jagged rocks,
jamming spray through holes they'd eaten.

2.
We walked a trail at Eight Dollar Mountain—
where gold miners found hefty nuggets, where ground absorbed
bodies fallen in the Rogue River Indian War.
The boardwalk led us over underground streams seeping into fens
of Darlingtonia, not yet in bloom when their bulbous heads
would stretch tight above leaves with throats waiting to trap flies—
now dark shriveled knobs, unsettling beside radiant meadows of Camas,
their little lavender petals open to let delicate yellow pestles
take hold of spring's sun.

3.
We drove the slow road through Stout Grove,
strolled the trail of soft bark among ferns unfurling
from winter, touched a redwood's insides
freshly broken—half-trunk splintered shafts
thrust into branches unable to stop their fall.

Patty Wixon's poem "Early April" features several stops on a recent car trip to Gold Beach, Oregon. Wixon's poems have appeared in several literary journals and anthologies. Her chapbooks include *Airing the Sheets* (Finishing Line Press, 2011) and *Side Effects* (Uttered Chaos Press, 2014). She is a long-time poetry co-editor for *Jefferson Monthly*, Jefferson Public Radio's program guide. She lives in Ashland.

Scott T. Starbuck

Earth Like the Deck of a Ship

Inuits say the sun's position has moved
and tongue drifts changed from north wind
to east wind. That is the real news.

This reminds me of the Luiseno Legend
"Before This Land" about when
"darkness and storms descended"
[. . . .] and "Uu-yot led his people to higher ground
and all were saved"

or talking to a 2000-year-old insect-and-
fire-resistant redwood
just before sunset near Crescent City
about her view of blue planet homo sapiens

or an old timer who said
"Maybe there is a spaceship you navigate
with an electric guitar.
In the 60s we made songs like that."

Thomas Rain Crowe wrote about Scott T. Starbuck's latest book, forthcoming from Fomite Press, "*Industrial Oz* may just be the most cogent and sustained collection of quality eco-activist poetry ever written in this culture, this country." Activist Bill McKibben wrote, "*Industrial Oz* is . . . rousing, needling, haunting." Starbuck was a 2014 Friends of William Stafford Scholar at the "Speak Truth to Power" FOR Seabeck Conference, and will be a 2015 writer-in-residence at Playa near Summer Lake, Oregon. His blog *Trees, Fish, and Dreams* is at riverseek.blogspot.com.

'Buckwheat Bob' Harrison

The Freeze

It was mid-November when The Freeze came to southern Oregon, as it did to the whole northern Pacific Coast. I had spent most of two winters in the Northwest, so I thought I was an expert on climatic conditions in that part of the world, and I was sure that it didn't usually get very cold there. Wet and miserable, yes. Co-o-o-o-l-d, no. According to the locals, the coldest it had been in years was about twelve degrees above zero.

Mara's kids were off visiting somewhere, and our house was really cold. It was a huge one-room with a loft. There were cracks and holes in the walls, and it had a totally dysfunctional stove. When you stoked it enough to do any good the roof would catch fire and I'd have to scoot up the ladder with buckets of water, if I could find any water. Ice doesn't do much good. Mara and I got so cold that we retreated to the Little Funky Egg Company. There was an easy and a hard way to get to the Funky Egg, across the river from Canaan, from where we lived.

The shortest and most direct way, a distance of about two miles was to walk to the river with your packs, guitars, and what all. If you could find enough rocks to jump to easily, you were across and on your way. If not, you would have to take off your boots, roll up your pant legs, and struggle, through the icy water and sharp rocks, carrying all your gear, to the other side.

If you couldn't cross the river you had to walk south about one and a half miles in the opposite direction from the Funky Egg then cross the river at the green bridge and walk all the way to town, several miles. The Funky Egg was full of crashers when we arrived, and we began thinking that it would be nice to get away from people for a while. Part of the reason that the Egg was so packed, was that four or five folks from down the Illinois River had been staying for a couple of days, and the rest of the place was filled with everyone in town who had run out of firewood or companionship. The threat of cabin fever was real; let's go to the Egg and party on, dude.

The folks from down river were ready to go back home to the Carrot Claim, a beautiful meadow on Soldier Creek. My girlfriend Mara and I decided to hitch a ride with them, to visit friends who lived on the top of

Horse Mountain, a half-mile above the Claim. This would be an adventure because this is rugged mountain, deep canyon country.

The reason we decided to make this journey was that Mara was especially close to her Aquarius sister, Rebecca, who was living with a notorious outlaw named Donnie. The desire to visit her, combined with the social pressures of hanging out waiting for the end of the current cold spell, probably shoved us over the edge. So Mara decided she wanted to visit Rebecca. It was the middle of winter, snow on the ground, and we were going twenty-six miles down the River Road, a dirt and mostly single-lane track along the steep Illinois River canyon wall. We didn't know how we were going to get back home, but it seems that we trusted our karma a lot back in those days. We knew we might have to make the return on foot, when it came time to go back home and pick up the kids.

The decision to make this trip seems especially strange to me now. It was snowing, cold as hell, we were hippies in redneck country, and we didn't have any money. We had the slightly dubious prospect of getting down river by riding in the back of an open pickup with a bunch of deep-woods maniacs, being driven by a major lunatic by the name of Big (and big he was, indeed), at night, in a snow storm. Why were we doing this? To go visit some more really crazy lunatics. Cabin fever must have been a terrible thing that winter.

We loaded our packs, containing among other things, three gigantic Buckwheat Bob's buckwheat pancakes for emergency supplies, sleeping bags, and my guitar, into Big's pickup. Then we wedged ourselves in among three other people and all the freight that could be stowed into the back of the truck. Part of their trip to town had been to get supplies. We started our fifty-mile sojourn. As we started down the road it started snowing for real. Big drove until the snow got so deep that we were losing traction. After we almost slid off the road into the canyon, he stopped and put chains on. I felt slightly reassured, seeing that we actually had chains. Then I saw Big tighten the chains with a length of binder twine, and my newfound confidence evaporated. However, there's not much you can say to a longhaired, six-foot, two hundred and forty pound mountain man except, "Right on." Also, I was not into piling off and walking thirty miles back home. So we took off.

Now, the road down the river is one lane of dirt and rock. And mud and snow. But at least it gets a lot of vehicular use, and has a pretty solid bed. However, when you get near Briggs Creek, about twenty miles down the road, and make the 270-degree turn onto Old Glory Road, you start up a steep grade of soft mud. Not many people use this road, especially in the winter. At this point the anxiety began. It was still four miles to Soldier Creek and you couldn't forget the binder twine holding the chains on. Big gunned the engine and slewed around onto Old Glory Road, with those wheels whining. It took us almost five minutes to pull up that 300-yard grade.

I certainly was not looking forward to having to abandon the dubious shelter of an open pickup bed and try to push the truck the rest of the way up the hill, knee-deep in mud. But we finally made it to the top. After that it was a fairly easy drive to Soldier Creek and the Claim, whereupon the pickup gasped its last breath (drive shaft or something), and there she may be to this day, for all I know. This abrupt arrival signaled the end of the good part of the trip, though of course we didn't know it at the time. We got there feeling just a little bit colder than an iceberg after dark in a snowstorm, but in one piece. The news that greeted us was that there was no one at the Claim. Everyone must have gotten tired of the weather and/or run out of firewood, and decided to ride it out in town or visit people who had firewood. I guess it is time to explain how folks lived (or managed to survive) in the bush back then.

Before I moved to the mountains, when my thoughts turned to fantasies of living in the woods, I thought that once you got out there you were there. I soon learned that there were actually various levels of "out there." First off, there were the people who moved to a small town, rented a motel room on the highway, got welfare, probably dealt a little marijuana now and then, and partied and had a good time. This would seem like the bush to someone who was from, say, Culver City, California.

The next level would be people renting farms and having extended families, communal situations, a bit away from town. Although the communal groups worked very hard, both at keeping the physical trip together and avoiding killing each other during the long wet winter, their community social activity was recognizable as somehow related to Western civilization as we know it. The next level involved mostly squatters who lived near the communal groups and either camped or built shanties out of whatever they could scrounge or steal. They pretty much lived a life of non-comfort, but expended a minimum of sustained physical labor for profit.

The last group included people who, for one reason or another, wanted to live way out in the boonies, where they might have to walk a number of miles to the closest store and then back home, carrying a lot of weight on

their backs, in sometimes very hot and sometimes very cold weather. Some of them had vehicles, which made things a little easier, but many of them did not.

These bush hippies were a mongrel horde: some were escaped city hippies, some city street punks who somehow strayed into the woods; the latter were mostly invited by the escaped city hippies who were trying to straighten them out and show them the good life. Some were paranoid survivalist types, some fugitives from justice as we know it. Some were old-time miners. This was a strange but generally fun group of people. On occasion they could be dangerous. The folks we were visiting fit well into the latter category of types.

We had never made this trek in winter before, so it was a new experience. The Claim was along Soldier Creek, which joined Briggs Creek about a quarter mile downstream. Briggs Creek fed into the Illinois River. There was a small, reasonably flat shelf on the side of a mountain ridge, with fertile soil for growing, and of course there was plenty of water. Up the side of the hill was a frame house constructed by some miner long ago, and several people currently lived in it. This time it was in a bit better state than it was the last time I was there. Betty and I slept (or tried to sleep) inside the cabin one rainy summer night, under a leaking roof. I mean really leaking. Everywhere.

Two couples had built shacks near the creek. Pete had built a pretty nice, small dome structure, while Tim had thrown up a dirt-floor shack. We learned that Donnie and Rebecca were not in their cabin on Horse Mountain, as we had thought. They had evidently run out of firewood and come down to spend the winter in an old shack, a short way down Soldier Creek. We found them just about frozen to death, with an inadequate stove and no room for anyone else to stay. Rebecca had blankets hanging from the ceiling in a vain effort to hold some heat near the stove. After we visited a while they suggested that we go stay in Tim and Carla's cabin. They had gotten smart and gone to town.

As we entered Tim and Carla's shack, it was evident that the owners had been gone for some time. The place had holes in the walls, of course, no insulation at all, dirt floor, and the stove was a squat half of a 25-gallon barrel, cut off and stuck in the ground. And no firewood. Obviously we would have had trouble getting warm, even if we managed to find wood in the dark. The only thing to do was to take off our boots, climb in bed, and

pull the covers over our heads. The bed was a plywood sheet on a board frame with unrecognizable pieces of foam here and there. The whole thing was really clammy and vile, with about twelve blankets of various lineages piled on the bed. They obviously hadn't been washed in a long time. We spent a miserable night, but at least we didn't freeze. Looking back it seems that over the last couple of years, I had spent several miserable nights at the Carrot Claim.

In the morning we got up, chewed some frozen pancake, and discussed how we were going to get the hell out of there. While we were musing about this, Pete and his lady arrived in his jeep. Pete and I had never been friendly but I sure was happy to see him. We lived our life by choice and I would not expect anyone to help us unless it were an emergency. Pete poured us some coffee and we warmed up a bit before starting back to town. I learned a bit about woods plumbing from Pete that morning. His exposed plastic water pipe was frozen solid where it was above the ground. He got a can of white gas and poured it generously on the pipe. He said, "I've heard that gas will thaw water in a pipe."

He lit the gas and sure enough, within a few seconds the water started running, a trickle at first, then completely free. White gas is so volatile that it combusts right away, and will not melt the pipe. I was impressed. Several years later I heard of someone who tried it on pipes under the floor of his house. It didn't work quite as well. I don't know if he had insurance.

This was the second time that Mara had been down the river. Last summer we had walked the whole way, the weather had been near a hundred degrees, and she had just about died of heat stroke, struggling down the road. Now it was just the opposite. Although in later years Mara earned her living as a tree planter, which is one of the toughest and most miserable jobs there is, at the time of this story she had been in the woods for less than a year. She was in terrible shape, and could see no reason to change that condition.

Before we left home, one bone of contention I felt very strongly about was that she should wear pants when we were in the woods. There are too many problems with skirts. I had been very insistent that she wear Levi's on this trip, but instead she wore a long Levi skirt, slit up the sides so that she could stride normally. This is fine for walking on flat surfaces, but it ain't worth a damn for climbing over rocks and logs. We decided that we would just have to walk back to town, and hope we could hitch a ride somewhere along the road. There was about two feet of snow on the ground. Our destination was Mar, Walt, and Cilla's place, about nine miles back toward town. If we followed the road back to Briggs Creek and then up River Road, the way we came in, we would have to walk about eighteen miles, but at least the pickup and Pete's jeep had cut a trail coming in. Three miles back down Old Glory Road, then three more miles just to get back parallel to where we were now. There was an old logging skid trail that cut from the claim to the River Road, which would cut about six miles off the trip, but it would mean breaking trail for about two miles. I finally decided to cut across rather than going back and around, mostly because I really hate retracing steps. And there I sat so patiently, waiting to find out the price I had to pay to get out of going through all these things twice. Thank you, Bob Dylan. This philosophy has gotten me in trouble more than once in my life.

We started across the meadow, with snow up to our knees. Mara got stuck, trying to get over the first log we had to cross. I was reflecting on that goddamned skirt and gave her butt a little kick. Not hard, just a sort of nudge. She turned around and shouted, "What the hell are you doing?" I said that I was just getting it out of my system early, and hoped she would listen to me next time. Fat chance. We struggled through the snow. I was able to find the way easily, because of course there were no trees in the middle of a skid trail, which had at one time been a road. We finally staggered onto River Road and took a little rest. The sight that greeted us was really beautiful, with the canyon and trees covered with snow and ice. The Illinois River way below us was frozen clear across in some places. The sky was leaden, though there was a bit of sun shining through. The fact that there was some sun bothered me a bit, because it doesn't take too much sun to go snow blind, or so I'm told, and we didn't have sunglasses.

We discovered that we had another problem, potentially worse than cutting trail. The wet surface of the road had melted and re-frozen, which left a layer of ice. This made it almost impossible to walk without slipping and sliding and expending a great deal of energy. Mara was at a particular disadvantage, because she was wearing her only boots, cowboy style, with no tread. That plus a skirt frozen to the waist must have made it a particularly unpleasant walk for her.

Soon after we started down the road, a redneck and his wife came slowly by us in a jeep, on his way back to town. He must have taken a Sunday drive to see the sights. We stuck out our thumbs, and he drove right past. That was the last car we saw that day. I was really angry with that citizen. I told

Mara, "If I had a gun I would shoot out his tires, then we could all walk back to town." Somehow we made it to our halfway point, exhausted, cold, and tired. We found our friend Mar and a lady we had never met before, named Ginger.

Ginger had on a thin coat and was really in bad shape. She had arrived recently from Montana with some dude named Cosmic, who seemed to be absent. They got blown away by the cold in the Big Sky country and headed for the coast, shedding their cold weather clothes along the way. She said it was colder here than Montana. I still believed the temp was in the teens at night, and maybe the high twenties during the day, but it sure seemed colder than that to me. Of course no one had a thermometer, telephone, radio, or TV, so we had no idea how cold it really was.

We spent that night in Walt and Cilla's cabin, a dome shake house that had holes in the walls. Having holes in the walls seemed to be getting a little repetitious. But by staying close to the tin stove until bedtime we kept reasonably warm. When we awoke in the morning, I volunteered to start the fire. The stove was about five feet from our pad on the floor, so I got up, naked, and started getting the paper and kindling together. I would do this any morning, all winter long, even if there was ice on the floor. It was kind of macho fun seeing people freak out watching the lunatic. However, this time there was obviously something wrong. The cold was terrible. Halfway through the job I shouted, "Jesus Christ!" and jumped back under the covers. I must have been an icicle. I guess I got even with Mara and her skirt that morning. I would get warmed up a little then jump out of bed and work some more on the fire. I finally got it going, on about the fourth trip out from under the covers. When I finally warmed up a bit, I got dressed and stepped into my gumboots. I almost fell on my nose when I took the first step. My boots were frozen solid to the floor.

We made a breakfast on almost the last of my giant pancakes, and started on down the road. Only twelve miles to Selma, and civilization. The traveling was slow that morning, obviously. I had to wait for Mara quite a bit, and encourage her to keep going. I forgot to relate that along with the other problems with that road, it did a lot of up and down. It starts at river level, and then goes up about seven hundred feet then back down to river level. It does this several times. Just how many I could have told you that day.

We finally stopped to rest at the last big turn before descending from the

mountains into a long, lush valley several miles short of Selma and Highway 199. We sat down on a couple of rocks and finished the last of the pancakes. I struggled up, but Mara was about at the end of the line. She said she couldn't go any farther. I got to play John Wayne. I shouted at her, "Get up and start moving or I'll kick your ass up through your mouth every step from here to Selma. I mean right now." I always wanted to say that to somebody. It worked, she struggled up and we slipped and slid for about a mile more. We stopped and looked down into the valley and saw a fox bounding along in the snow, a magical moment. Miraculously, a man and his wife stopped and let us ride into Selma in the back of their pickup. By now, even in the horrible cold, riding in the back of a pickup was luxury.

When we finally reached the Selma store, we jumped out of the truck. Actually, we didn't jump. We stepped very carefully to the pavement. If we had jumped just then I think we would have shattered into a million pieces. We thanked the good Samaritans sincerely and trudged into the store's coffee shop and ordered coffee. Hot. We looked at the clock and it indicated that it was 3:45 in the afternoon. As we were savoring our coffee someone walked into the store and said that it had just gotten up to fourteen degrees above zero. Startled, I queried further and they told us that it had gotten down to negative sixteen degrees the night before. Then I understood why we had such a miserable time.

We now had a good news bad news situation. True, we had escaped the jaws of discomfort in the dreaded canyon and made it to Selma, Oregon. Selma, however, would never be mistaken for Los Angeles, for example, when it comes to settlements. The commercial district consisted of the store we were in (which fortunately had a lunch counter), a post office, a Laundromat, and a Chevron gas station. Home for us was still about twenty miles away, only ten of which were on the main drag, Highway 199. So now it was about an hour before dark, and we certainly didn't want to try to hitch after dark. Among other things this was redneck country, and Takilma was far off the main track. Our situation was still precarious. We walked out to Highway 199 and stuck out our thumbs. Luck seemed to be with us and we got a couple of quick rides. We reached the Funky Egg, our original starting point, before dark, just about forty-eight hours from the time we had left.

The party and wall-to-wall people were still going on when we arrived, and we discovered that the kids were still off visiting and wouldn't be back until the next day. We were just about beat, but we felt much better after several hours of heat and various intoxicants provided at the party in the Other (the other house at the Funky Egg). There were two houses, Robert's home, the Nebulous of Andromeda, and the Other, which was home for everyone else. Mara and I woke up refreshed the next morning. When the temperature finally got up to zero degrees, everyone went outside and we had a small ceremony. After leaving a message for the kids that we would be home, Mara and I walked and hitched to Black Michael's mining claim the next morning, about four or five miles, and couldn't make it any farther. We walked through his door and caved in. Michael didn't do things by halves. He had the Franklin stove cranked up max and it was like an oven in there. Several of the Godzilla Wrecking Company, Michael's extended gypsy family and performing company, were in the room, as well as three or four of the Gunslingers, .357 magnum pistols and all. Everyone, it seems, had been driven indoors by the weather.

Michael smiled and waved us in. We told him about our journey, and he started pouring water pans that had been boiling on his stove into his oversized tin bathtub. He told us to strip off while he got the water together. To get us started, he poured us each a mug of peyote tea he had brewing on the ubiquitous stove. We complied with his order to drink up. As we sipped the brew and luxuriated in the streaming tub, finally getting the freeze out of our bones, it seemed well worth the misery to have this kind of comfort and hospitality at the end of the trip. I wish I could elaborate on what happened next but I can't remember. Well, you gotta play hurt. Later that afternoon we walked the road about a mile to our cold, cold house.

The weather finally broke and it started raining, but it took several days for our cabin to become unfrozen. As I said before, our dysfunctional wood stove was inadequate to deal with sub-zero temperatures, and the propane stove fittings had frozen and had gas leaks. We couldn't use it at all. The most discouraging sight, however, was the sink full of dirty dishes in the frozen dirty water we had left behind at the time of our flight. The whole mess was frozen solid and we had to look at it until it finally got warm enough to melt the ice in the sink. Gross.

'Buckwheat Bob' Harrison. Lived by his wits in the Northwest woods for 15 years. Returned to tech work with the State, running a graphics, desktop publishing, and video production unit for the next 13 years. Now retired, he devotes himself mostly to performing and recording music. His memoir, *Hippie Tales of the Northwest Woods*, is now available from Hillcrest.

John Noland

Earth Music

I am standing on pristine sand within a sea cave, a sea cathedral. Monoliths and pinnacles of dark rock rise around me, leading the eye up and up into the open sky. There is a small doorway into this sanctuary and a small doorway out of it. These doorways have been carved by the sea. Soon the water will rush through them again, drowning this place where I stand.

Here huge stones catch the wind, muting it, giving it voice, soft and haunting as the calling of mourning doves at twilight. It mixes with the surging crash of the sea. This music is both ethereal and earthy, like ballads sung by ancient birds when the earth was young. It haunts and thrills and whispers. It stirs in our veins, rhythms that go back before forgetfulness, back to First things when such songs were sacred. Our bodies ache to answer, for bodies have their own memories and their own hungers, their own ways of knowing and remembering. They echo a moment, a shadowy grace granted by blood's antiquity.

Sea Riddles and Doorways

There is something hidden in sea fog and darkness, and it calls to our oldest selves like geese call across the October moon or coyotes howl in the desert. Here on the beach, it also speaks in the language of animals—a low, guttural cacophony of voices, ancient chants wrapped in time and seaweeds, and redolent with undersea caves or the first smell of cedar. It is found in constellations that mirror the great, deep choruses of whales. It is also hidden in the small piece of driftwood that has ridden the tides from other places, other times. And it is the flicker of light caught in the raven's eye as he hunkers like an old man over a driftwood fire, warming his hands and counting out the day's magic.

John Noland lives and writes near the ocean in Coos Bay, Oregon. He has published in *Chicago Review*, *Orion*, *Nature Writing 1999* edited by John Murray, *Georgetown Review*, *Seattle Review*, *Laurel Review*, *Jefferson Monthly*, and other publications. His most recent chapbook is *Midwestern Trees and Shadows* (Finishing Line Press). A previous chapbook, *This Dark Land Where I Live*, won the Kulupi Press' "Poetry of Place Contest," and his chapbook *The Caged and the Dying* won the 2012 Gribble Press Chapbook Contest.

Rhonda Lynn

Fiber Arts

I discovered fiber art and felting about 4 years ago. I fell in love with the sustainability and versatility of the renewable resource that is wool, and continue to be amazed by all the wonderful things I can create with it.

The natural beauty of Southern Oregon inspires each piece I make and is a reflection of the respect and care I wish to bring to the land through this amazing medium. I am constantly amazed by the depth and texture of the finished pieces and also by the unlimited creative possibilities and sustainability that the medium provides. I am able to create a wide array of textures, colors, movement, feeling and function while using what nature has already provided.

When combining recycled and repurposed fabrics with wool, I am able to direct the flow of surface design and textures through the choices of fabric densities and colors. Textiles provide a unique vehicle of interpretation with their tactile nature, vibrant color and endless variety. Instead of paint, I select fabrics to get the desired effect. The happy accidents of working in this medium give results that can be challenging and pleasingly unpredictable. Materials, techniques and themes are a starting point for each piece and the flexibility of the process allows me to change direction and intention as the piece evolves, takes shape and "becomes."

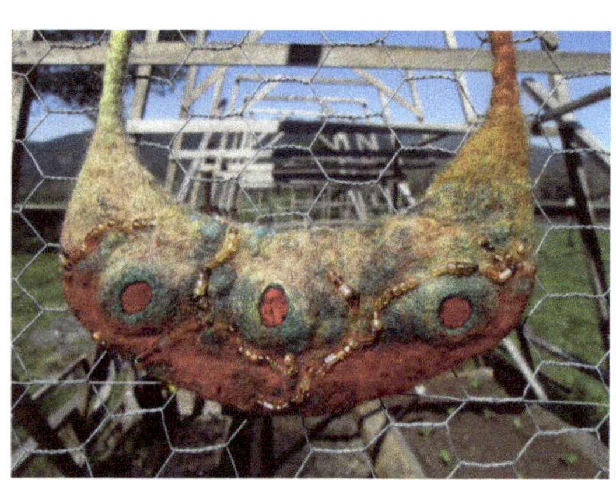

Time and creation have become the leading edge ideas in how I not only approach my art, but how I approach life as well. As I apply these ideas to my artistic endeavors it has helped me to see that every part of my life is a creation in which I must allow room for attention to take root. This has made me not only a better fiber artist but a better creator and artist of my life.

Rhonda Lynn says, "I became a dedicated felt maker after becoming enchanted with the magic of the medium. From wool, soap and elbow grease, one can create beautiful pieces of wearable art." She focuses on one-of-a-kind "Art to Wear" that is environmentally friendly and infuses upcycled fabrics. In addition, Rhonda conducts workshops in felt-making. Her latest endeavor is conducting classes in middle schools focusing on the sustainability and many uses of wool in our daily lives. Find her at facebook.com/MustBFelt and inspiredfelt@gmail.com.

Lilyana Rain

Wonder

I wake up, and I **wonder**. Life is a crazy thing. Humans even more. How we adapted and created? How we look? Have you ever **wonder**ed over this thing that we call hair? Dead cells coming together to create a strand very weak alone yet strong together. Kind of like humans. Or our eyes, all different colors. Our skin different textures and colors that cover meat which covers bone. Blood, how it's blue but bleeds red. And how some see colors, how some can't? Think of it: if you were blind, deaf, without feeling or senses, your life like a black hole, no end to the dark. I am getting off subject. But I **wonder**, I **wonder** a lot.

I am not a quiet person. I am, quite frankly, the opposite: always something to say, though I notice everything about a person, all their ticks, emotions, looks. I have ideas of what their future might be like. I am no prophet, but I notice everything. I had taken on photography thinking I could capture that, but now I know you can't. I seem to always overthink things, things that most people dismiss and don't think about. Like death. Death. The biggest mystery. What happens? Were do we go? Heaven? Reincarnation? Ghosts? All e other farfetched ideas. Or do we just die soul in body together die? We will never know, not until our time comes, when we see the *light*–then the biggest mystery of life will finally be answered and we will not have to **wonder** anymore.

How were we created? Atheists and others believe it's just a fluke we just ended up here. The *Big Bang*. Others believe of Adam, Eve, God, Evolution, goddess and so many more. What do you believe? I am still uncertain. Religion is also a weird thing; it determines everything I suppose. Like I said before, we will never know so all religion is a way you chose to live your life, your lifestyle. Do we all come from the same *god*? If so, then wipe away the hate. Does everyone have their own? And that's their creator? Our inner god? Mysteries, but that's what makes life fun–the mystery of it all.

This earth and this life form didn't come with a *Book for Dummies* or instruction manual so we are screwing up a lot. This is not how it was meant. We can't go on like this. With crime increasing, pollution, war, violence, natural disasters, population incensement, global warming. Something's going to have to happen. A thread's going to have to break. This world is going

to have to change if we would like to spend more time on it or it will happen. So what's going to happen? God(s) knows where we're heading. At this rate I don't even want to know. Who would? If you could know everything, every little piece of knowledge. The entire history? It might sound nice for a second: knowing how we were created. And you probably wouldn't make mistakes. But the catastrophe would be too much for any living soul to handle. If you didn't die from heartbreak you would die of the weight of the world. Killing you slowly. The most painful death.

It's sad to grow up in a world and see your future taken away in the hands of carelessness, to **wonder** what will be there for my children. What life from here on out will I live? Each day could be our last, every breath could be followed by silence, but we, we have lived day by day and not worried about tomorrow for too long; you can control tomorrow by making a change today. It's time to think about years to come. I don't want to live in a world where teenagers are killing each other on the streets daily, where adolescent suicide is at a high peak, where the air poisons your lungs and your food is killing you slowly. What is this? What have we created, what have we done? We have indebted ourselves and it's time, it's been time for awhile, and each day comes and goes yet each day it gets worse. These are some things I **wonder**.

You know the term *scientifically proven*? Nothing is proven, not a single possible thing–hell we aren't proven. To be proven is to know and we know nothing. As much as a newborn baby. New born baby. As alive as you and me though much more free. No idea of its life or *life*, no clue of this world, the joys and horrors. All a mystery. Newborn child most venerable but most free. Variability we all are at a time of being the most venerable. But variability comes with a price, that price being the ability to be Free. And to be Free is to Live. So it's an all-in-one package deal. Sadly, as it seems we, we are not free–our minds are trapped and our eyes are blinded and our ears are lied too; the illusion we have been fed that we are free is hilarious, just damn funny because that–that's bullshit. Someone once said "fear is not real, it's all in your head, but pain, pain is very real." So that's the note I'm leaving on . . . Is it all in your head?

I **wonder**.

Lilyana Rain is a homeschooled 14-year old singer, actress, musician and writer. She loves sharing her voice with the world and she has an album coming out in late July 2014. You can find her music at www.youtube.com/lilyanarainmusic or join her newsletter to stay in the loop by emailing Lilyanarainmusic@gmail.com.

Kindi Fahrnkopf

Thunder Warning

Thunder erupts from a malevolent sky
A grey day's blanket of heavy smoke crumbles
Boils up with charcoal, mauve, yellowish mushroom clouds
Thunder heads grumbling, tumbling on the mountain top
Then boom, crash, crack of dry lightening jolting down
On the painfully dry land, already ravaged by so many huge fires
Consuming all life
Red Flag warning goes up in declaration of emergency conditions
People beware-it is too late now if you haven't prepared
Things are coming too fast now; accelerating destruction.
The weather means to punish man-whether or not we try to stop it
Mother Nature is raging mad
For all the abuse she suffers
For our Earth; which would not exist without the lifeblood water
Is being polluted beyond the point of return
We have passed the tipping point.
And now only a miracle could serve to anoint us with the balm of
Fresh water in a land of dying refugees.
With the cries of children echoing the land,
How can mankind hold his head high?
Do we even know yet, what has happened?
We are entering a time of the Third World War.
A global war just as Nostradamus predicted over four hundred years ago.
The USA blindly marches into battle, behind a curtain of deception
As the leaders of the world create and sell weapons of mass destruction
They seem to allow the evil among us to control the destiny of mankind,
whilst reassuring us all that they have our best interests at heart.
I can hear the thunder warnings in the sky.

Rain

I am finally feeling you; rain
Spattering on my roof, falling urgently
Kissing the ground with passionate pain
From a long-sought union of earth and sky
We waited so long for your arrival
On parched ground, crackling underbrush
We walked in confusion of understanding why
The drought had taken the lush, green from us
The lakes had fallen into murky, algae pits
Strangling life, coughing up dust in fits of fear
We know we are water babies
We cannot live without you, even shed a tear
We are just sad children, waiting to be healed
I am finally feeling you
Moon over river as yellow lights up my upstairs room
The super-bright rays infusing me with feelings
Upwellings, in my deepest core
Colliding with lucid dreams
Putting me under water
Did I float on you once?
Did I roll over your waves in a reed sailboat?
Once upon an ancient ocean current, singing
A song of love for the sun
Always guiding me
I feel your undulating swells rocking me to sleep
Mother Ocean, I feel as though you are washing over me
Your fierceness fizzling into the foam
Rising into the spray and meeting the misty, rain clouds
I am finally feeling you; rain.

Susanne Kindi Fahrnkopf was born in Germany and grew up in Southern California. A hippie, flower child of the 60's, Kindi moved to Cave Junction in 1979 with husband Jim and 2 children to open the Cave's Cobbler shoe repair & Birkenstock shop. She raised 4 children at her Takilma home and works as a Bookkeeper. Kindi has been published in 7 poetry anthologies. Her book, *Takilma Tales: The Hippie History of Takilma, Oregon*, is a vivid history of the little-known community of Takilma. Learn more at takilmatales.com.

Kay Elaine Ekwall

In The Soft Silence. . . .My Heart

Mother earth opens her arms to me....
warm is her embrace,
"You've returned, my child"
and I cry tears of gladness.

I enter her womb, her icy streams...
which cleanse my dusty feet....my soul.

My salty tears mingle
with the life forces rushing to the sea
from out of her depths.

She decorates my body
with unearthly music of pines,
whispering, sparkling lights...
...flickering through the trees,
I am covered with diamonds and rubies
reflecting their glory.

The emerald velvet on her branches
heals my spirit...my open wounds,
I am no longer bleeding.

In the soft silence......my heartbeat
throbs with the sounds of water...
rushing as it nurtures all life,
....as I do, too.

I give silent thanks for all those before me..
who have fought valiantly
to keep her forests standing
the paths, saving her pristine meadows,
the valley......so fragile.

Vibrant carpets of flowers greet me...
Indian Paint Brush, Lupine,
Buttercups and Mountain Heather,
they delight my heart as I take inner
pictures, imprinted forever.

Wistfully.....not wanting to ever leave
this tranquility, I do...

Calmly putting my life in order,
priorities in proper places.

My voyage into the mother, as always…
bringing me home.

Kay Elaine Ekwall lives in O'Brien, having moved from northern California in 2003 and immediately felt like she was 'home'. She didn't know that some ancestors had lived here before they became Californians; her great uncle having been a representative for the state of Oregon. Kay's poetry site is 'Poemotions" and she has many photograph websites, the newest being Rough and Ready Creek.com. She loves being able to walk out the door, or drive close by and get shots of nature and critters so easily. She was first published when she was in college in 1963, and has since been published in online sites, in newspapers and more.

Troutish Longings

I could be a trout, no doubt,
Speckled, long, and sleek,
Spend my summers in the
cold,
Basking in the creek.
Frigid waters ‘cross my back
Anglers cast their bait
For a rainbow from the brook
On the banks they wait.
I could be a trout, no doubt,
But I don’t think I will
I don’t like the looks of hooks
Or the water’s chill.

Dave Dunbar

Dave Dunbar is a graduate of West Virginia University at Parkersburg and currently resides in Prospect, Oregon. His poetry has appeared on or in *The Seismic Thread:A Northwest Storytelling Project*; UW Baraboo/Sauk County's *Spirit Lake Review*; UW Barron County's *The Red Cedar Review*, and West Virginia University at Parkersburg's *Gambit*. He has also self-published free form books of multiple genres including his favorite, the science fiction comedy *Station 24* and *Revenge of the Space Smelt!!!* 2nd Edition.

Kelly Waldin

My tribe is getting smaller.

Memory shows me snapshots of you in black and white,
in a time when you were young.
Youth and marriage, playing roles and bearing witness to
a change of seasons, with joyful births and times of sorrow.

My tribe is getting smaller.

Riding a bike, with a push and a smile, trying to remember
what was said, just a smell, or a moment of the feel of your
hand in mine crossing the street.
Dreams and death, always watching and awaiting its
appointed time and space to share themselves.
Hoping for tears with no outcome of grief, as my
tribe is getting smaller, and you are missed.

Kelly Waldin resides in Westside Takilma with her partner Waves. "It is your mind that creates this world."

Night Visions

The purpose of the Night Visions series is to reveal, or uncloak, patterns of nature that are either not readily discernable during the day or do not have the same visual impact. The only tool I use is my camera flash — no time exposures - so that only those aspects of natural patterns that reflect light are revealed in the photo. The resulting images are often quite startling. In some cases, the raw image is the final one. In others, I may make some adjustments of brightness, contrast, and color saturation to create the final image. Finally, I write a "praise poem" as a complement to each image, so that each finished piece in this project consists of image-plus-praise-poem.

Great Expectations

Garbed in the frills and frippery and finery of yesteryear, this decaying bride awaits the groom that never did arrive and never will. Wrinkles have consumed her face, as waiting her life: hope turned to dismay, youth to dust, gentility to jest. She remains, scorned but proud, unbendingly, in her gown of startling virgin white. Waiting, waiting for life's fulfillment.

Night Wind

Rushing through secret interstices comes the wind of night. Primordial in nature, both predating and outlasting humankind's existence, it is a thing of magic that passes, unfelt, through highly evolved bodies such as ours. But rooted beings - we call them lower forms — must bend and rend before that fierce assault, leaving raked and twisted traces for the morn to come.

Revealed in Flight

Nothing showy, muted in your floral affect. Indeed, shocked by the brutal attack of the flash, you lean away, attempting to recede again into the secret, murmuring society of the dark.

Spellbound

Your sinews are locked in contorted embrace, spellbound reminder, perhaps, of some decades old transgression. Were you unwilling witness or wilful perpetrator? What forbidden sight did your eyes behold? What sacred law was shattered in the wake of your careless momentum? No matter which, you are bound by the chains of some unhappy past. The gods are cruel and unforgiving.

Originally from Boston, Anita Savio has lived in many parts of the U.S., and in Mexico and Canada as well. She writes, "Although four photos and accompanying poems of mine appear in this issue, I consider myself to be, at best, an amateur photographer, and a poet only when great need arises. I have also worked as a reporter and freelance journalist. Among my current and creative endeavors is my lively blog on thoughtful nonfiction: www.brainybooks.org. I invite you to pay photos, poems and blog a visit!"

Rich Norman

Poem for Paul

Tides caress a distant shore
And days, melt over-joyous, far
Away and distant seen is light
Brought at long to gently find.
But closer still the hand and eye
See more and much to fill in sight
And sound the shore of rocky cleft,
Now pummeled down to dust bereft
The tender sight from distant length
Is crowded rock and brittle beach
And wandering in sands of heat
The meek do shawl and hands do reach
So drawn is sight and sound to pitch
Of knowing need and empty stitch
And suture bound to time from past
To beauty's hand but stitched in lash
The scorch of heat burned skin and flesh
Of man his time is tender spent.

How to hold of care and so
The road not up but down into…
Release the handle, turn no wheel,
Can hands twice blistered hold to feel?
The honest eye says no, not true
I have but lost and found no truth
Hungry beating stains heart's breast
Must find in tender rapture's fleece
Another hand, an eye to see
To hold the gut, wound bled and cut
A sack and pouch spilled into dust

And dirt but swallows blood and sting
The eye, the throat is parched within
Who but sorrow might damp these eyes?
What but tear, can tear unbind?

To you I hold but candled heat
Kindled black and bitter deep
To open pain and spill black blood
Release and find our wound full runs
As ocean spilled on rocky shore,
Tears glaze shadows held afar
Running water bringing tide
The shore but close in light cast right
Pain is anchor, buoy, light
I will show you…here is sight:

An eagle tucks its wings and finds the earth
Its sight set firm beneath
Crashing through layers of tangled heat and wind,
Spitting headlong toward annihilation
An arrow of death and purity
Unthinking and sure
Snatching blood and flesh from the skin of the earth
Proud and unthinking,
Rising upward as light and death,
as life and the feast which is won.

Warm and gracious is the noon which spills
From the unthinking arch
Slow as honey might become light
Teasing its shades from the heart of heat and white
Now unshattered
Poured up from the eye as golden broth and thick light
A new sun and noon find the day unfurled, unthinking
New and wise
…alone, waiting and perfect…
As silence.

Snow collects as delicate diamond flakes descend
Her coat soon covered in sparkling moonlight
How perfect is the sight
The wolf shrouded in cold's delicate fingers
Sleeping, freezing, … quietly … suffering
Awake! The shudder before all beautiful deaths
Spitting frost and glittering chips of ice
…into the moonlit dark
Dancing and falling is death,
A beautiful ghost descends as a prismed cloud.

Soundless is the fact
A whisper's breath heard,
A leaf descends and is nestled into the grasses
Can you hear this, so fragile is her soul
Alone and at one with her,
No man is near,
No woman has known,
The perfect splendor
The most fragile peace
…new, perfect and delicate, is its unfolding.

Black tar and asphalt, can not consume light,
Mirage spilling upward, dissipating and vanishing
…once alive as shimmering light
Unchained over heat
Dancing before all endings…shimmering and rude
Unafraid and vanishing, spilling upward…
Brash and singing, silver and shouting,
Dancing… and vanishing: as life.

Rich Norman is the founder and editor-in-chief of *Mind Magazine* (www.mindmagazine.net) and *The Journal of Unconscious Psychology and Self-Psychoanalysis*. A writer, newspaper columnist, and musician with degrees in philosophy and music, he is the author of books and scientific papers spanning philosophy, psychology, neuroscience, verse and fiction, as well as a contributor to the Ultranet, and the Prometheus Society journal, *Gift of Fire*.

David Lorenz Winston

Nature Photography

David Lorenz Winston

David Lorenz Winston is an award winning photographer, internationally recognized for his nature photography. His crisp winter landscapes and stunning images of trees enhance art and photography collections around the world. More than 300,000 posters have been published of his image "Solitude," an image of a zigzag fence and tree taken after a fresh coat of snow near Philadelphia. David publishes *The Winston Eye*, a weekly photoletter featuring his latest work. Learn more at davidlorenzwinston.com.

Full Moon Meditation

There is a little man inside me
he is skinny
narrow
hungry like a straw.

He has opinions where none are needed
has needs where none are wanted
he is slippery and never shuts up.

This man, I reside within him
he is callous and fearful
ruined like the earth

Dallion McGregor is a writer, artist, and cartoonist living in southwest Oregon. He's currently working on his first graphic novel while attempting to buoy his heart lest it be thrown to crocodiles. More of his work can be seen at dallion.com.

Finding Me

Speak through my atmosphere of spinning wheels
Clarity among the buzzing and humming
Of too many thoughts dizzying my perception

Sound out the droning of constant experience
Breathe coolness into my hot temper
Calm my overwhelming

Take me back to that river
Where the purest secretions of living water
Trickle into a pool of my hope for peace

Where an earthen cliff covered with delicate ferns
Tells me it's safe here
And towering ancient trees hide me in their wisdom

Where my children swing out and let go
Into crystal beauty surrounding them
Giving them clarity and courage

Where I submerge myself in the peacefulness
Of a world wet with life enough to leave my darkness
And come out, for my little ones to see, beautiful and clean.

Writing

I am writing and I am happy
Pen to paper
Thoughts to page
Mind releasing my life story

The waters of my expression I have dammed too long
The processing of my days by the movement of my hand
My brain is forming shapes and lines of letters becoming
words that are my euphoria

I feel like an artist, a conductor, a poet, a writer, a dancer
with words.

Summer Wolf lives in southern Oregon with her husband and 4 children, including Isaac Wolf and Juliette Wolf. She is a full time mom with a career in the health industry that keeps her busy but allows her to work from home. On the rare occasion she finds a moment to herself, she might write something of her experience or observation with some hope of sparking a flame in someone, while reminding herself of her own fire.

Juliette Wolf

Great Big Cedar

The cedar, higher than other trees,
with warm breeze passing by.
Oh the fresh potent smell
Of the Great Big Cedar.

Isaac Wolf

The Cave

The cave is so dark I can hardly see
I'm resting on a rock listening to the dripping water.
I am surrounded by peacefulness in the shadow hole
Where sightless fish dwell.
This is where I want to be when I'm stress filled
Then, when my mind is clear, I get up
And move towards the light.

David Newell

Eyes Slide Off of Me

I don't know what
it's like to walk around
being *Beauty* –
eyes glued on you all
over

I walk around *Ugly* –
eyes slide off of me –

isn't it annoying
when you bump into things
and the eyes pop –
and there's eye stuff
all over

The Poem Said

sometimes all you want to do
is fill an empty space, said the poem

like Procrustes you chop
my arms and legs to fit
your square frame bed

why not put the ocean in a spoon
and if you really want
go tuck yourself in

My Life

My life is a ripe plum –
complete –
it has a worm in it.

I thought it was
a butterfly once –

it gnaws
and leaves a tunnel inside

with nothing in it
but butterfly shit

I Gotta Go to the Ocean

I gotta go to the ocean
if only to see it die

See the gulls last wheeling
flight

Hear the humpback's cry –

See the incredible
Living fish's
Last swim
by

The Poem Said

I'm always around
said the poem
beneath your perceptive world,
underground, in a well

anytime you can throw
a bucket down
when you need me

anytime you remember me
said the poem
anytime you want to carry
an old bucket

David Newell lives in O'Brien, Oregon. He is a wood carver and artist who spends his extra time playing banjo for his marionette gnomes and fairies, and throwing spears with an atlatl. Oh, yeah, he makes the banjos, marionettes, and atlatls. His first full collection of poems, *The Poem Said*, is set to appear in 2015.

Susan Gustafson

The Date to Hell...and Back Again

This took place in the late 80's or early 90's. I had been looking forward to an event at the Dome School, anticipating a fun and refreshing night of dancing to the music of Walt Richardson and the Morningstar Band.

My husband Craig hadn't decided yet if he wanted to go or not. Then he asked me to go with him to Kerbyville Ghost Town; he had heard there was something going on there. I was torn as I didn't want to miss the dance but he hadn't asked me out on a date for a while so I reluctantly agreed. Then it turned out he wanted us to ride on his recently acquired motorcycle. I don't like motorcycles; they feel unsafe. But off we went, and I froze because it had been so long since I had ridden on one that I forgot how to dress for it.

We arrived at the Ghost Town to see rows of motorcycles; it was clearly a biker event. It was very crowded inside, thick with smoke and nearly impossible to get served. There was a band playing but the atmosphere was about as different as you could get from Dome School: I couldn't dance by myself and Craig didn't want to.

I was wondering how soon I could ask to leave when out came a woman on stage. She did a strip tease which elicited the expected catcalls and whoops, but nothing out of control; just the whole thing was pretty tacky. Then out came a man doing a strip tease and women rubbed themselves all over him! Tacky doesn't begin to describe it; I was embarrassed for womankind. Finally we left. Thank God.

Another freezing ride; I was thinking, okay, it's still early enough. I can still go to Dome School. But to my horror, we pulled in to Red Garter! Oh my God! Would this nightmare never end? Evidently not. I was getting the feeling that Craig didn't want me to go to the other dance.

So we hung out for a while at Red Garter. He seemed to want to make a night of it. Funny, even though we went there about once a year (in between Dome School dances) there were the same people we saw last time, with the same tobacco smoke.

After what seemed like forever, we finally left, for the freezing ride home. I was so disappointed by our date that I went and changed my clothes and said, "See you later, I'm going to Dome School." Craig couldn't believe it. He said, "You're kidding!" But I just had to leave.

I arrived shortly before midnight to wonderful music and got to dance to the last song. It was enough. It felt like such clean energy, it was pure happiness. I divested myself of the negative energy from the earlier part of the evening, and felt cleansed. Then somehow, magically, everyone in the room formed a circle holding hands. We just stood there for a while, feeling the good energy. It was an incredible, warm and loving feeling. I was home again.

What a perfect ending to the date from Hell.

Susan Gustafson has lived in Cave Junction since 1978. She works at The Dome School and also makes flower remedies for people and animals which assist with emotional healing and personal growth. She and Craig have long since figured out what makes them happy.

R.I.P. Blaze

Life has taught me many lessons, many I did not want to know.
Like how to love unconditionally, and how to let it go.
Passions slowly fading, hearts must drift apart.
What I'd give to feel that fire exploding like the start.
Your kiss stunned me with poison, like a widows dance with death.
She cried "I'll never stop loving you" as she watched his dying breath.
Her heart, it keeps on mourning, a wound that never heals.
Watching a part of you die, no one should know how that feels.
Tears flow freely, a river with twists and turns.
I loved him with a passion, a fire which embers still burn.
A numb and fading soul, exists with only a breath.
I may not make it longer dear, for soon I'll join you in death.
My days just aren't the same dear,
I long to feel your touch.
I thought it may be easier if I just took a little too much.
My heart, slowly fading as I picture your beautiful face.
Not too much longer dear and I'll be in your embrace.

Dedicated to Blaze Broberg's friends and family

Angela Graves moved to Southern Oregon from Oklahoma 11 years ago. She has managed Bagel Junction for the last 3 years. She notes, "I have been writing since middle school and need to do more of it." She enjoys hiking with her husband and three kids.

Annette McGee Rasch

Of Women and Mice

Mice scamper throughout my earliest childhood memories. To teach us kids about gentleness, my parents employed two of these tiny creatures. Skippy and Sylvester soon became full-fledged family members and spent most of their time in our pockets.

Our dog Corky once made a fast grab, poking a tooth through Skippy's eye. My Lord, how the blood gushed. We all hovered and cried while Daddy performed mouse surgery: torching the tip of an ice pick until red hot, he cauterized the tiny eye socket. Ooh, that was nasty, and a vivid life lesson about how fast play can turn to pain. But Skippy bounced back with great aplomb, also demonstrating how quickly a creature can shed trauma, transcend handicap and get on with the business of life.

Many years later mice re-entered my world en masse, when my mother's illness prevented her from spending much time outdoors. To keep our shared passion for wildlife alive, I'd developed a deluxe bird-feeding station on our huge front porch. The mice came too, but we didn't care. Facing Momma's mortality had suspended the rules of reality. Even after fall's chill set in, on her "good" days, bundled in blankets and tucked into a big soft chair with a hot cup of coffee, she'd enjoy the day's drama.

While songbirds flit among the feeders, brazen mice intent on fallen seeds wove between our snoozing old dogs lying around the porch. Sometimes my sisters and friends mentioned the porch mice, well OK, they brought it up frequently. I'd stay (uncharacteristically) quiet and wait for them to talk about something else, grinning, if they couldn't see my face. Comfortable with the conspiracy, Mom also developed selective hearing.

You see, our 'mouse watching' had become sort of a hobby. So damn cute, how they'd poke their little heads out here and there. So carefully, they'd wriggle and scoot, humble but bold – surely shouting out to the world in some frequency now silent to us: "Please let me live! I don't want much." And we often admired their technique. The mice performed great acts of balance and acrobatics, sometimes with Luke, the Great Dane, staring intently, just inches away.

Bold Stellar Jays shrieked onto the scene several times a day, scattering beeping finches, hopping nuthatches, and the chickadees, who pecked around the porch floor beneath the feeders. Every so often a mouse and a chickadee found themselves in direct competition for the same fat sunflower seed. They'd make eye contact and after a moment's impasse the chickadee usually flew off with the prize; though occasionally the mouse would charge and win the day. The hummingbirds never cared what was going on, they'd dive-bomb throughout it all to get at their feeders and favorite flowers. Only the squirrels had to wait for the humans and dogs to go inside before mopping up the day's offerings, and on breezy days, the sleeping dogs' noses would twitch when the impatient squirrels crept near.

Many chores weren't getting done in a timely fashion during this period, including hauling the garbage away and turning the fresh compost into the piles. We rang the welcome bell and the mice answered. Even in the barn, I'd poke my head over the top of the dutch-door and there they were, kicking back, sipping margaritas.

In each location the local mouse collectives developed unique operating procedures. For example, in the afternoons, some of the barn mice utilized our dozing horses for cover. Using binoculars, we'd observed a mouse crawl out from under the barn, pause, then make a mad dash over to a hoof, where it huddled while plotting its course to the nearby pond. One morning I found a completely flattened mouse…

Then in late winter all mouse watching was suspended when my beloved Momma passed on. Soon after her wake and everyone had gone home, a big snowstorm knocked the power out and enveloped my world in a silent white shroud. That storm was perfect. Taking to my bed, pitching into sustained sleep – my first in years – nothing much caught my attention for several months.

Come spring, the mice rather nudged me back to life. Opening the front door, yup, there they were, on the porch. Heading out to feed the horses, hmm, they're everywhere… With fresher eyes, my place looked like one of those rat temples in India. How'd I not noticed the mice crawling up the side of the house, rooting around overgrown gardens, skipping down the driveway and hopping about in the pastures? It was shocking to behold their sheer numbers – while I'd slumbered; they'd multiplied.

But even then, it was difficult to get past my amusement and sentimentality – until they showed up inside the house, on the kitchen counter!! That tore it. A girl's got to draw the line somewhere.

I felt incredibly awake. While I'll always treasure the time Mom and I had shared watching wildlife on the porch, this freaky multi-species frat party was over. But then, the dilemma: I don't kill healthy animals. Still, it was war. So. I purchased some live traps and gently captured 50 mice in the first week. Inside the house, I eliminated their food sources, and thankfully, driven by hunger, mice are easy to catch. Those who got wise to the traps were left with only one option: the spillage on the bottoms of the parrot cages.

Trying to prevent contact between these two species, I'd slathered Vaseline onto the cage legs. This resulted in a great show one night. A mouse tried to make the climb, but kept sliding down. It finally gave up and hid behind a bookshelf, but then, after a few moments, the mouse galloped toward the cage – and jumped! Sailing right between the cage bars, it landed neatly inside. Just before slipping beneath the newspapers lining the cage floor, Petrie, the Macaw, cocked his great blue head sideways and said "Hi" to the tiny creature. Then Barney, one of the dogs – who incidentally looks a lot like Richard Gere – came over and licked the Vaseline from the cage legs, his ears perking up each time the mouse rattled the newspapers. It was really too much.

While the dogs were lousy hunters; the 15-year-old house cat found moves she didn't know she'd had. The mice were her fountain of youth and she drank of them greedily. It was gruesome, the way she'd toy with them, and impossible to watch. So when mortally wounded, I'd quickly euthanize the creature and lay it on a tree stump out back – to the delight of the neighborhood ravens, one of whom would swoop in, snap and swallow in a single movement. Anyway, the mice were soon evicted from the house. Easy living for the porch mice was over as well, after I'd relocated and downsized the bird-feeding station; and finally, making that overdue dump run and maintaining my compost pile sealed the deal.

So what became of all the mice?

My prisoners (about 200) were comfortably relocated to riverfront property at the end of the road. I'd left them with food, water and a big thick blackberry patch to call their new home. They'd have to rough it, but the view was good. I knew I'd miss them.

I'll always remember those days of disconnection and transition, how the mice helped keep humor in the picture. But few of us get to duck from reality for long and it was also the mice who brought me back and forced me to pay the piper. And who's the piper? Had I played a flute, perhaps they would've just followed me down to the river.

Big Brothers for Cows

If I were in charge, Earth's "New World Order" would be staffed with environmentalists, children, teachers, scientists, storytellers, animals, spiritual people, healers, plants, counselors and dog trainers.

This global leadership would exclude lawyers, C.E.O.'s, lobbyists, high-level government officials, generals, popes and politicians. For these folks, I'd designate a special social rehabilitation program: The Big Brothers For Cows. Or simply: The B.B.F.C.

But before getting into the B.B.F.C., let me say that the New World Order wouldn't tolerate chemicals, GMO's, sloppy nuclear activity, old-growth logging, fracking or indiscriminate burning of fossil fuels. Bans on human activities that increase global warming, pollution, habitat destruction and extinction would be strictly enforced. After all, humans have evolved plenty enough to better utilize their minds and far less of Earth's flesh and blood to satisfy the hungry practical needs of civilizations.

There'd just be one rule: if any proposed human activity hurts other life-forms, you can't do it – not without super-solid justification that passes the scrutiny of bio-regional boards comprised of enviros, scientists, gardeners, kids, etc.

Though obviously, the immediate end of planes, trains, ocean tankers and gas-guzzling vehicles would cramp global bio-restoration during the transition to better technologies. Yet the wetlands can't wait – they need reviving now! All those pesky dams must be removed, not to mention the badly located cities, leaking landfills, electrical lines and fiber optics that require extraction from the flesh of Our Mother.

No worries – we'll simply call the B.B.F.C. That's right, the Big Brothers For Cows! Let the revolution begin!

Since the New World Order decides it's wrong to breed, imprison, torture and then butcher animals so humans can consume their flesh – the meat industry is sunk. This moral decision is backed by sound economics: it takes ten to twenty pounds of grain to produce one pound of beef – an awful waste of land and water.

But what to do with all those excess cows? Some suggested we just eat them and be done with it; but others argued that surely a cow deserves its life too. So an eight-year-old came up with the solution.

Got a big dam removal job? Just call the B.B.F.C. This wonderful social rehabilitation program pairs sterilized cows with presidents, generals, lawyers, dictators, C.E.O.'s, ect. And not just these folks; the sentence is bestowed upon anyone who fails the New World Order's 'Responsible Power Broker' test. (The test was diligently constructed by a sub-committee comprised of teachers, mothers, ecologists and plants.)

Thus they go forth, in twos. Picture it! A president and his cow, followed by a disgraced C.E.O., and of course, his trusty cow. Every sanctioned F.B.I. Agent? Yup, they'd each get their own cow.

In fact, every effort is taken to help each member of the B.B.F.C. find their very own special cow – as this bonding results in their most significant personal relationship for the entire five-year program! (Complete with twelve steps.)

Off with their cows they'd go, loaded with hand tools, into the sunset, toward the dams, to start their righteous task by removing the concrete from Earth's arteries. The Raven Brigades would monitor compliance to Proper Cow Treatment Standards. So if some dictator with an attitude problem abuses his cow, a big noisy black bird would croak the violation to the New World Order. Cow Abuse buys you another five years in the B.B.F.C.

Only fully rehabilitated power brokers, extractive industry addicts, rabid developers, war mongers and chemical pushers would be allowed back into general society. A truly kinder, gentler world, featuring exquisitely wise use of Earth's gifts would emerge. And there'd be a lot more birth-control…

You'll have to read my campaign platform (oops, I mean my novel) to hear the rest!

Annette McGee Rasch is a freelance writer who lives in the Illinois Valley. Raised by naturalists and animal lovers, Rasch is also a dog trainer and wildlife rehabilitator who possesses vast experience with multiple species. She also spent decades working as an environmental activist and is a perennial student of the sciences. Her writing reflects her love for and knowledge of the natural world.

Michael Spring

Cobra Lily

near the bog
we stand above the snake-like presence
of cobra lilies

I place my finger
on a leathery leaf
that secretes
a sexual slip of syrup
for insects

inside the body of the plant
inside its membranous head
two flies have climbed in
and now twitch, intoxicated
in a pool of liquid

if this cobra lily
represents our love

then the insects trapped inside
are last night's erotic
words and heavy sighs
transformed into flesh

their bodies
slowly absorbed
into the plant

Michael Spring is the author of three poetry books and five chapbooks, His most recent book, *Root of Lightning*, was awarded an honorable mention for the Eric Hoffer Book Award, and his chapbook, *Blue Wolf*, won the 2013 Turtle Island Poetry Award. He lives in O'Brien, OR. He is a natural builder, a martial art instructor and a poetry editor for three publications: *The Pedestal Magazine*, *Mind Magazine*, and *Cobra Lily*.

Savanna G. S.

Teardrops from the Clouds

The Rain falls from the clouds
It hits the roofs, "Bang, Bang, Bang!" very loud.
Children jump in the puddles.
While others stay warm in the house, giving cuddles.
Rivers keep flowing and flowing,
And the wind keeps blowing and blowing.
Wild animals are hibernating in a peaceful sleep,
And the clouds are still crying a very loud weep,
But when the drops are stopping,
The children end their hopping.
The sun peeks through the trees.
The birds sing in the air, and "Buzzz," go the bees.
A colorful streak of light makes an arc through the sky,
As the rain and the clouds go, "Goodbye."
The children all sing and dance,
While Heaven looks down at them with a cheerful glance.

Savanna G. S. writes, "I am 12 years old and live in the Rogue Valley. I really love to draw and write books and stories. I want to be an author and artist when I grow up. I also like to write poems for many occasions."

Alan Laurie

Winter Solstice Mandala

Winter Solstice Mandala   Alan Laurie 2003

Electric Mandala

Alan Laurie has been an artist all his life. He can recall at age 3 finding joy with a red crayon, ruler and some sort of paper while drawing what he knew was a large letter "L", and then, satisfied, running back outdoors to play. His experiences include festival poster artist, television courtroom artist, and political campaign graphic designer. He has lived in Takilma for 13 years and his graphic art skills are behind many a familiar local logo. His "Cubist Cub" is on permanent display in front of the Grants Pass Art Museum on G Street. Alan is Co-Editor/Publisher of *Takilma Common Ground*.

I Like Coffee

The flooded river,
same color as my cappuccino,
but loud and fast,
takes crates 'n branches
and . . . green basketballs? . . .
no, pumpkins!   vines 'n all,
uprooted, on the field trip
of their life!

It all goes down today!

People who own
basements and antiques
are wet 'n upset,
but not me!   I like the way
water spins
around tree trunks.   I like
change!

Redwood Vision

"The redwoods, once seen, leave a mark or create a vision that stays with you always." —John Steinbeck

My first redwood forest planted a vision in my mind
of a house connecting earth to sky.
A bedroom in the basement roots, pitch dark for sleep,
where dreams feed on thick river silt.
A kitchen in the lower trunk, eye level with black bears
foraging salmonberries in misty understory.
Azaleas make their own pink light in deeply dappled shade.
Higher in mossy branches, I sit on a slanted porch,
eyes shut to fully hear dissonant warblers and thrushes,
percussion of woodpeckers and wingbeats of hovering
flycatchers. Closets are crevices in rough, grainy bark
holding scrolls of poems and maps.
I climb a stairway of erratic burls up to a crow's nest
above the fog where I might almost see the ocean,
were my vision not scorched
by the giant needle-splintered sun.

Weeder Geese

The small white geese are easy.
I need only raise my right hand
to make them swerve left,
or my left to make them move right.

The fields are fenced to keep the geese
eating Bermuda grass,
clover, and horsetail
between pungent spearmint rows.

Goslings work best, enjoying food
more than sex. A hungry goose
will dig nubs of grass, even eat the roots.
A fighting goose is a feast.

I remind myself they are meant to be used.
But as I stumble down my muddy path,
and pause to unfold a silver wrapper
off a sliver of gum, I sometimes see

wild geese flying a ragged victory V,
feel twinges of pain in my sore shoulders,
and sense a shadow in the sky
raising an arm behind me.

The Rabbit

After the Seder,
on the empty highway, suddenly
a rabbit.   His body thuds under my car.
That fast.
I saw him clearly in my headlights—
an adolescent brown cottontail
with elegant profiled ears.
One exquisite pause
ended his life.

I falter under bright lights, too.
Because I think *should I go, should I stay*
I'm hit by my hesitation.

I'm not a neophyte at sacrifice.
I know if I leave my husband
I'll have to leave alone—no room
for apple trees in my car,
and no friends will come with me,
not even our beloved cats.
And I know that freedom is a harsh desert,
harder than an Egyptian brickyard.

Haven't I learned
plague after plague,
slaughter after slaughter,
there's never time
for bread to rise?

Four Senryu for the Beaver

Muddy beaver tail
whacks the shin of the sign post,
flings chocolate batter.

Beavers work off road
with the highway repair crew.
Hard hats, flashlights, jaws.

Last night the beavers
got into the coffee urn.
Up 'till noon, pissed off.

Overnight, the woods
became a pasture bristling
with sharpened pencils.

Sara Backer, an Oregonian for 15 years, now lives in New Hampshire where she teaches at UMass Lowell and leads a reading group in a men's prison. Her poems have received three Pushcart prize nominations, two Best of the Net nominations, and two nominations for the Best New Poets anthology of 2015. Her recent publications include *A cappella Zoo*, *Allegro*, *Carve*, *Crab Creek Review*, *Gargoyle*, *Hermes Poetry*, *The Pedestal*, *The Rialto* (UK), and *Turtle Island Quarterly*. For links to her online publications, visit the bio page of sarabacker.com.

Scott Simpson

If . . . (Doghouse)

If I can just find the spot on my wife that I can find on my dog
That spot that makes the leg kick around like a science-experiment frog
I'd tickle that spot and laugh 'til I cried
'Stead of walking 'round this lonely ol' yard like somebody died

The sheets on our bed would be set into motion
The neighbors would knock and ask "What's the commotion?"
I'd gain her respect and I'd earn her devotion
If I could just find that spot ...

If I could just tickle my wife on that spot that I found
And wear her plumb out 'til she stopped making sounds
She'd leave me in peace to do some of my thinking
And wouldn't complain about all of my drinking

She might even lie tired in the corner like my devoted Tick Hound
And chew on a pig's ear or an antler she found
If only my wife could be that happy just chewing on bone
Instead of chewing my ear off over the phone

Why I'd be happy too and not way out yonder here
And we could peacefully get ourselves on in our years

If I could just tickle my wife on that spot that I found
Get her leg in the air going 'round and 'round
She might lick my feet – even between the toes
Lick the wax from my ears and the snot from my nose

She might lick my wounds to help them all heal
Become happy with scraps and the occasional meal
Then I'd scratch on her backside whenever she reared
Scratch the top of her head and behind both of her ears

If I could just scratch at that spot and make my wife all twitchy
Go hard at that spot as if it were itchy
It just might be the cure that would make her not so … serious …
We could both find Nirvana – walk around all delirious

If I could just find the spot on my wife that I can find on my dog
That spot that makes the leg kick around like a science-experiment frog
I'd tickle that spot and laugh 'til I cried
'Stead of walking 'round this lonely ol' yard like somebody died

And I'd be her man again and not just a louse
She might even let me back into the house

Scott Simpson lives in Selma, OR. He can be found hosting the very popular Wednesday Open Mic Night at Wild River in Cave Junction, OR. He is a novelist, poet, and song writer. Yes, he has dogs. He can be seen running the mountain paths with them. If you think you've spotted Big Foot with a guitar, or a tennis racket (i.e. the best looking and well-groomed Big Foot ever seen), chances are you've spotted Scott.

Rory Forsythe-Elder

Wolves

These creepy, cruel carnivores snap at their prey, a deer, with terrifying precision.
Blood splatters against the ground as the deer fails to survive.
The wolves munch on the fallen animal, satisfied with their kill.

Rory Forsythe-Elder is 10 years old and likes eating ice cream. He lives off-grid in the woods of the Illinois Valley. He does not like beets.

Deborah Ann Dawson

Lady of the Lake

Door in the River

Silent Among the Reeds

Deborah Ann Dawson is a Southern Oregon native who grew up in the Rogue Valley and majored in Art at what is now Southern Oregon University. In 1978 she was the first woman to receive the Outstanding Senior of the Art Department Award. Deborah has focused on Drawing and Watercolor for the last 26 years, including teaching drawing and watercolors. She moved to the Illinois Valley in 2001 and opened the Artful Being Studio the next year. She also became an Artist in Residence for the Southern Oregon Arts Council for 3 years, teaching drawing and watercolors to thousands of Southern Oregon's elementary school children. Learn more at deborahanndawson.com.

Kathryn Velho

Anabel

Crying with her head against the worn hardware floor, Anabel silently strokes her doll's blond hair. She remembers waking up in the morning and seeing that doll for the first time lying next to her. While she ran out to thank her mother and father for her unexpected present, she noticed that they were gone. Now she was here, sick and hungry waiting expectantly for her parents' return even though it has been longer than a month since they left. Unlike Anabel, her parents were living their dream in Spain, 4,713 miles away.

* * *

Lily wakes up in a dark room. All she remembers was stopping at a rest stop on her way back up to Oregon after visiting cousins in California. Slowly she stands, her legs wobbling, and scans the room. When her eyes adjust to the darkness, she notices strange scratch marks along the walls, holes and stains on the wood flooring, and a lone doll lying stranded in a corner. Walking across the room, Lily picks up the doll to examine it. As she turns the doll in her hands, she notices bald spots and white marks on its skin. "Signs of love," she concludes.

When she puts the doll back in its place, its hand comes completely off and a long sharp knife takes its place. Standing completely still, Lily stares at the armed doll in horror. Suddenly it stands and starts to move on its own holding out its knife, coming toward Lily. Lily jerks backward and hits her head on the wall behind her. She falls to her knees as the doll stops next to her and tilts its head upward–looking at Lily with one cracked eye. It stands still for a moment before plunging its knife into Lily's thigh. After the doll retracts its knife from her leg, a steady flow of blood begins to flow, forming a scarlet puddle on the floor.

More dolls appear crawling out of corners and climbing out from underneath floor boards. Too scared to scream, Lily sits trembling while holding

her bleeding leg. Stiffly the dolls walk to Lily who frantically backs herself into a corner sobbing. All at once the dolls lift their hands which fall from their writs in unison and are replaced by a variety of sharp objects. Expecting the end, Lily looks away.

She notices a small girl standing behind all the dolls which freeze in place as if awaiting a signal.

"Do you want to play?" the girl asks. Tilting her head to the side, her black hair falls to one side, revealing a very thin and pale face.

"No not really!" Lily sobs.

"I'm Anabel," she says plainly. "Are you scared?"

"Yes," Lily admits.

"Good," she says with the same expressionless face as before. "You're gonna be my new doll."

"WHAT?" Lily screams before slumping against the wall unconscious.

Lily wakes in a blindingly white room with Anabel hovering over her. Anabel wears a torn white nightgown which is stained with blood. Upon seeing Anabel, Lily jerks upwards then screeches in pain as she clutches her crimson leg.

"Do you hate me too?" Anabel asks.

"YES!" Lily screams. "I just want to go home!"

"Don't worry," Anabel consoles. "You will love me soon."

The room fades back into the room where she first woke up and she is again surrounded dolls. Anabel stands in the same place as before, staring intently at Lily. Anabel tilts her head downward. A shadow covers her face so all Lily can see is her mouth which is curved slightly upwards. Abruptly the dolls lunge at Lily and plunge their knives into her. Lily screams as blood splatters against the walls and floors, drenching the dolls and Anabel who seems unfazed by the desperate wailing.

Lying with her head against the kitchen floor, Anabel strokes her new doll's red hair while humming a lullaby her mother used to sing to her. She forgets her parents who left her to die years ago and cuddles her doll under her chin and smiles.

"I love you, Lily," she says softly.

Kathryn Velho writes, "I am currently 16 years old, I love writing scary stories, reading all kinds of books, and drawing Anime style pictures. I go to a charter school and I've lived in the beautiful rouge valley Oregon all my life."

Kailen Forsythe-Elder

Taped Pumpkin

Kailen Forsythe-Elder, age 5, says, "Say this: Kailen knows how to ride a 2-wheeler bike. And I run fast. I jump off a swing, landing on my *feet*. Albert and I are friends. Kamy and I are friends."

Acknowledgments

Several of the works published in Cobra Lily were previously published elswhere:

"Redwood Vision" and "Weeder Geese" by Sara Backer previously appeared in T*urtle Island Quarterly*. Her "I Like Coffee" first appeared in *ArtSpirit.*

"Full Moon Meditation" by Dallion McGregor and "My tribe is getting smaller." by Kelly Waldin previously appeared in *Takilma Common Ground*.

"Cobra Lily" by Michael Spring previously appeared in his book *Mudsong.*

Also, Ryan Forsythe would like to thank Michael Spring for springing for ten bucks to get us a web domain. Not to be outdone, Michael Spring would like to thank Ryan Forsythe for giving him yet another publication credit for his poem "Cobra Lily."

www.ingramcontent.com/pod-product-compliance
Lightning Source LLC
Chambersburg PA
CBHW042013120726
47911CB00029B/907

* 9 7 8 0 6 9 2 4 4 4 7 4 0 *